Text copyright © 1995 Jeanne Willis
Illustrations copyright © 1995 Amy Burch

The right of Jeanne Willis to be identified as the author
of this Work and the right of Amy Burch to be
identified as the illustrator of this Work has been
asserted by them in accordance with the Copyright,
Designs and Patents Act 1988.

First published in Great Britain in 1995
by Macdonald Young Books

This edition published in 2008 by Wayland,
am imprint of Hachette Children's Books

Wayland
338 Euston Road
London NW1 3BH

Printed and bound in China

British Library Cataloguing in Publications Data available

ISBN 978 0 7502 5427 4

Wayland is a division of Hachette Children's Books,
an Hachette Livre UK Company

Jeanne Willis

The Story of
Florence Nightingale

Illustrated by Amy Burch

WAYLAND

1
The Battle of Inkerman

It was 1854. As the cold, November sun rose over the Crimea, the dirty blanket of fog and gunsmoke began to lift. The Battle of Inkerman was over.

Trapped under the carcass of a chestnut mare, Private Tom Wilcox stared in disbelief at the huddles of red and gold rags stretching as far as the horizon. Fourteen thousand soldiers lay dead or dying, and for what? The Russians were still inside Sebastapol, the British and French no nearer to victory.

Tom felt a sob rise in his throat. This wasn't how it was meant to be. The British army were supposed to be the finest in the world.

That's why he'd run away from home…to be a hero. To be a soldier in the Crimea!

He'd even lied about his age to get in. The only person he'd told his secret to was Alfie, his little brother, but Alfie must have blabbed.

As Tom marched proudly through the
streets on the day of the farewell parade,
he spotted his mother searching
frantically for him among the rows of
soldiers.

He'd wanted to call out, to wave, but he daren't. Instead, he beat his drum louder and louder in the vain hope that she might notice him, but his efforts were drowned by the stomp of marching boots.

Now he was lying on a battlefield in a strange country thousands of miles from home and he'd never even said goodbye.

Tom tried to roll away from the dead weight of the horse but he was too weak to shift her. There had been nothing to eat for days. As for the horses, they were so hungry, they'd started eating each other's tails in desperation.

The world began to spin. As Tom floated in and out of consciousness, he thought he heard the voices of French soldiers.

"Under the horse!" shouted someone. "Alors, c'est un petit garcon...why, he's no more than a boy!"

Tom felt a tremendous weight lifting from his body and screamed out in pain.

Then everything went black.

2
Hell on Earth

"Mother!" shouted Tom.

"Keep the noise down, will you pal," said a voice next to him, "you'll frighten the rats."

Through the darkness, Tom could make out the image of a lad not much older than himself, lying on a rough bench. His head, bristling with ginger hair, was resting on a pair of muddy boots.

"Where am I?" panicked Tom.

"Hell on Earth," grumbled the freckle-faced soldier, "in other words, Scutari Hospital…have a look at my arm will you? It's itching like mad…I'm Eddy by the way."

Tom rolled up what was left of Eddy's sleeve, peered at the bayonet wound and was almost sick. It was crawling with maggots.

"You should show that to a doctor," he said, screwing up his nose and letting the sleeve drop.

"Doctor?" scoffed Eddy, "I've been here five days and haven't seen one."

"Well, show the nurse," said Tom.

Eddy rolled his eyes. "You're joking aren't you?" he said, "there are no nurses. What kind of girl would come and work in a dump like this. It stinks. She'd have to be drunk as a skunk."

"But I need the privy!" said Tom, "I can't walk on this leg."

"What privy?" said Eddy, "listen, soft lad. They're full to overflowing. There's no mops, no medicine, no nothing…that's the army for you, pal." Eddy shrugged his shoulders and began blowing monotonously on a small tin whistle.

Tom rolled over onto his side. No
tears came, just small, hopeless sighs
that he couldn't control. Suddenly, the
whistling stopped.

"Hey, come on," said Eddy, kindly.
"Don't take any notice of me. I'm just a
no-good, scouse…I never meant to upset
you. It'll be O.K, honest."

"No it won't," said Tom.

"It will," insisted Eddy, "My mam reckons everyone's got a guardian angel that watches over them. I've got one... you've got one..."

"Really?" said Tom

"Oh aye," said Eddy, "the only thing is, mine's a lot prettier than yours. Mine's blonde."

"What's mine like?" asked Tom.

"Covered in ruddy freckles," said Eddy.

The two of them giggled like a couple of school boys. After all, out of uniforms, that's exactly what they were.

3
Guardian Angels

Eddy's mother wasn't entirely wrong about the guardian angels, or so it seemed.

Little did the boys know that ten days earlier, a very determined young woman called Florence Nightingale was seen marching boldly towards Scutari Hospital with thirty-eight of the best nurses she could find.

"Keep up, ladies," she said briskly, "there isn't a moment to lose."

"No indeed, ma'am," simpered Noreen, a plump little Irish nun, "we must get down to nursing the poor fellows straightaway."

Florence gave her a withering look. "The strongest of us will be needed at the washtubs," she snapped, "have you not read *The Times?* I hope you have a strong stomach, my girl or you might as well get straight back on the boat and take up flower arranging like my dear sister, Parthenope."

"Yes, ma'am," Noreen bit her lip.

"Don't go upsetting yourself," said Tilly, a bright, cockney girl who had befriended her on their rough journey across the Black Sea, "Miss Flo's bark is worse than her bite. She's got a heart of gold really."

Noreen snorted. "I'm serious," said Tilly, "her old lady wanted her married off to some toff. The family reckon it's a flamin' disgrace, her being a nurse, but I think she's done marvellous making it to the top like she has. Can't have been easy."

Florence put down her suitcase.
"Here we are," she said, cheerily. It was
all she could do to disguise the feeling of
horror welling up inside her as they
trooped into the hospital.

"Cor…what a pong!" whispered Tilly. "Gawd help the poor devils, they're packed in like sardines."

Holding her hanky over her nose, she picked her way through the rows and rows of sleeping soldiers.

"Quiet, Tilly!" hissed Florence, "they've little dignity as it is without your silly comments. Get to your rooms, girls. We are not to show our faces to these men until the doctors find the good grace to let us do so!"

Eddy opened one eye. "Tom!" he squealed.

"What?" said Tom, still half asleep.

"Pinch me!" said Eddy.

"What?"

"Go on, pinch me…to make sure I'm not dreaming. Look over there.. can you see them?"

"Who?…where?" asked Tom.

"In the skirts and hats!" said Eddy, excitedly.

By then, the nurses had disappeared into their quarters.

"You're hallucinating," said Tom. "Go back to sleep."

4
Heaven

Tom was woken by the clattering of a
metal bucket and the comforting sound
of a woman humming softly. At first, he
thought he was hearing things, but no, it
was Tilly.

She was on her hands and knees,
scrubbing the floor with a rag.

"Blimey, you're a young 'un," she said, smiling at him.

"Your hands are bleeding!" said Tom.

Tilly looked at them and wrinkled her nose. "Miss Nightingale reckons it's all this muck that's causing the tummy troubles," she said, ringing out the filthy cloth, "never mind me, when did you last have something decent to eat?"

Tom couldn't remember. All he'd had since he arrived was lukewarm greasy water with a few shreds of salt pork floating in it.

"Thought as much," said Tilly, "soon as I've finished what I'm doing I'll go to the kitchen and fetch you a nice bit of stew. Miss Nightingale says if the doctors won't let us nurse you, the least we can do is fix some decent grub and get you cleaned up."

"Could Eddy have some too?" asked Tom. "Only I'm really worried about him. He was all right last night but he looks terrible...it's his arm."

Eddy looked very pale. His eyes were closed and he was shivering.

Tilly sighed. "With any luck the blankets and sheets will arrive soon," she said, feeling Eddy's brow, "Miss Nightingale's sent to England for all manner of stuff...she's got friends in high places."

"Who is Miss Nightingale" asked
Tom, "is she a…guardian angel?"

"You could say that," winked Tilly,
"chin up, I'm off to empty my bucket."

While she was at the sink, Tilly heard raised voices coming from the doctor's quarters.

"I cannot believe you intend to amputate that young man's arm without chloroform. It's butchery!" insisted Florence.

"Madam, better to hear a man bawl lustily than see him sink silently into the grave," bellowed the doctor.

Shortly after, as Tom was tucking into the delicious meat and vegetables Florence had prepared, Eddy was carried into the crowded corridor on a stretcher by two bleary-eyed surgeons.

There was a glint of steel, a scream, then silence.

Suddenly, Tom wasn't hungry.

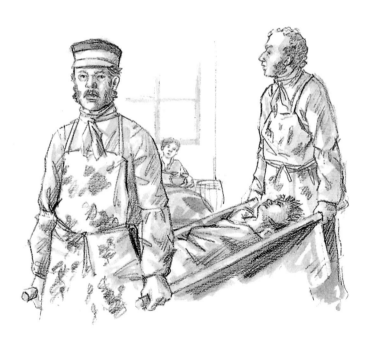

5
Lady of the Lamp

"Can you sit up for me, sweetheart? I've to give you a nice wash, a clean gown and see to your leg. The doctors have finally agreed you lot need a woman's touch."

Tilly put a fresh pillow behind Tom's head and plumped it up. The sweet smell of the antiseptic soap caught the back of his throat. It reminded him of his mother, standing over the washboard, scrubbing away at the shirt collars. He wiped a tear away with the back of his hand.

"Sorry, am I hurting?" asked Tilly, "only I've got to clean this wound, it's infected."

"It's not that," said Tom, "it's just...I just...I miss Ma and Alfie and I want to go home!" he gulped.

Tilly put her arm round him, "you didn't ought to be here in the first place," she said. "How old are you?"

"Seventeen," said Tom.

"Come off it," smiled Tilly, "more like thirteen...am I right?" Tom nodded his head.

"You'll be going home soon enough, Tom. Bet you tuppence ha'penny," she grinned. "Now how's my Eddy today?"

Eddy had barely said two words since his operation. He'd lost a lot of blood.

"Eddy, we've got clean sheets!" said Tom, "the medicine's arrived and the bandages and the angels...we're in heaven!"

Eddy managed a weak smile then he seemed to fall asleep again.

That night he had a violent fit. His eyes rolled wildly and he kept yelling things that made no sense.

"It's all right, Eddy," said Tom, trying to hobble out of bed. "Don't worry, I'll fetch Miss Nightingale."

"You're wasting your time, laddy,"
said the Scotsman in the opposite bed,
"that poor lass has been on her feet for
twenty-four hours. There's eight
hundred men needing her attention. She
can't do anything for your pal."

Just then, Tom saw the familiar glow of Florence's turkish lamp.

"What do you think you're doing out of bed, Private Wilcox?" she asked, "you are supposed to be resting that leg."

"It's Eddy," said Tom. "Is...is he going to die, Miss?"

"Not if I have anything to do with it," she whispered softly. Tom watched as she leant over Eddy's bed, holding his hand, soothing his forehead with a cool flannel.

It was as if Eddy was her only son.

6
Going Home

"I'm in love," announced Eddy.

"Who with?" asked Tom, swinging his mended leg backwards and forwards.

"With the lady of the lamp, of course!" he said, "with Miss Florence."

"Leave off, she's mine," guffawed the huge Scottish corporal, "I'd marry the wee lass tomorrow, only Mrs MacDonald would nay let me."

"She'd never have you, Jock," joked Eddy, "it's me Flo loves...she saved my life."

"More's the pity, you noisy young shaver!" boomed a major, "by the way, chaps, you'll never guess what the inspectors found fouling up the waterworks."

"A Russian?" sniggered Eddy.

"Only a blinking dead nag," hooted the major. He held his drinking glass up to the light. "No wonder the bally water tasted orf…mind you, it's like champagne now, since the old girl gave the authorities what for. Here's to Flo, chaps…Chin, chin."

"Anybody fancy a wee dram?"
suggested the corporal, waving a small
bottle of whisky in the air. Just then,
Florence swept into the ward. The bottle
disappeared swiftly back under his
pillow.

"Corporal MacDonald!" she said, firmly, "why don't you go and take coffee in the reading room? By the way, I have written to your wife, as you requested."

"Thank you, ma'am." The corporal looked suitably ashamed of himself until she had disappeared, then he blew kisses after her.

"Och, I could kiss her shadow," he sighed, "this must be the first army hospital in history where the wounded actually get out alive!"

"I'm getting out soon," said Tom, excitedly. Then his face fell.

"What's up?" asked Eddy.

"Oh," said Tom, "it's just that I wish I could tell Ma to expect me, only I can't…"

"Can't what?"

"I can't write, if you must know," blushed Tom.

"So what?" said Eddy, "Miss Nightingale will help you write a letter. She did one for Jock, didn't she?"

A few weeks later, little Alfie Wilcox ran into the parlour with a letter for his his mother. It was short, but to the point.

"Dearest Ma," it said, "I'm coming home. Your loving son, Tom."